CAPE PLAYS

CARITAS

ARNOLD
WESKER

CARITAS
A Play in Two Acts

JONATHAN CAPE
THIRTY BEDFORD SQUARE LONDON

FIRST PUBLISHED 1981
COPYRIGHT © 1981 BY ARNOLD WESKER
JONATHAN CAPE LTD, 30 BEDFORD SQUARE, LONDON WC1

British Library Cataloguing in Publication Data
Wesker, Arnold
Caritas.
I. Title
822'.914   PR6073.E75

ISBN 0-224-02020-X

TYPESET BY ROBCROFT LTD, LONDON WC1
PRINTED IN GREAT BRITAIN BY
R. J. ACKFORD LTD, CHICHESTER, SUSSEX

Dedicated
with love and hope
to my nephew
Jake

Author's note

I should like to thank the touring theatres of Norway and Sweden and Det Danske Teater of Denmark for generously commissioning this play.

I should also like to thank Professor Paul Levitt of the English Department of the University of Colorado for urging me to look into the world of anchoresses and in particular the scant story of Christine Carpenter.

The historical Christine Carpenter lived in the Surrey village of Shere. She became an anchoress in 1329. Documents have recently come to light revealing that the original Christine was immured, broke out three years later and then seems to have been persuaded by the authorities to re-enter her cell.

CARITAS

Note for translators

The dialect as in *Roots* and *The Wedding Feast* is from
Norfolk. I have not rendered everything in dialect. Simply,
'ing' is 'in''; 'and' is 'an''; 'that' is 'thaas'; and the rest is
peppered with the occasional 'hev' and 'hed' for 'have' and
'had'; 'bein't' for 'be not'; 'on' for 'of'; 'ent' for 'is not' and
'am not'.

Note for directors
This is a relatively short play, but the first and second acts
must run together.

The lighting for the first act dictates itself. For the second
act, although I haven't indicated it, the 'parts' being in the
main very short, they need to be divided by 'puffs' of light
fading in and out with sufficient darkness in between to
allow Christine to move into a new framed position.

This play was first presented by the National Theatre Company at the Cottesloe Theatre, London, on 7th October 1981, under the direction of John Madden. The designer was Andrew Jackness and the lighting was by Rory Dempster. The cast was as follows:

Christine Carpenter	PATTI LOVE
Agnes Carpenter	SHEILA REID
William Carpenter	ROGER LLOYD PACK
Robert Lonle	MARTYN HESFORD
Matilde	ELIZABETH BRADLEY
Henry	FREDERICK TREVES
Mathew de Redeman	PATRICK DRURY
Richard Lonle	
Villager Travelling priest Bailiff	PAUL BENTALL
Bishop's clerk Tax collector	JAMES TAYLOR

CHARACTERS

10 actors to play 13 characters

Christine CARPENTER	a young anchoress, between 16 and 21 years old
Agnes CARPENTER	her mother, aged around 40
William CARPENTER	her father, a carpenter, aged around 42
Robert LONLE	Christine's ex-fiancé, apprentice to William, aged about 20
MATILDE	an old woman, 60s
HENRY	Lord Bishop of Norwich, aged 50
Mathew DE REDEMAN	rector of St James's Chapel, Pulham St Mary, aged about 30
Richard LONLE	Robert's father
Villager Travelling priest Bailiff	*to be played by one actor*
Bishop's clerk Tax collector	*to be played by one actor*

TIME	July 1377 to July 1381

SETTINGS	
Act One	a composite set to include: the wall, altar and circular window of the chapel; part of the anchored cell wall and its grill window; a carpenter's workshop
Act Two	interior of anchoress's cell

ACT ONE

SCENE I

July 1377.

The interior of the church of St James in the village of Pulham St Mary, Norfolk; a carpenter's workshop; the window and part of the wall of the anchoress's cell anchored to the church.

CHRISTINE, *daughter of* WILLIAM *the carpenter, is about to be immured in the cell.*

Light slowly touches the opening in the wall. This is the first thing we see. Huge stones alongside, waiting to be put in place.

Light then touches the solitary figure of CHRISTINE *who stands before the altar, her back to us. We will not see her face till Act Two.*

Light next touches the carpenter's workshop where stand three rough but solid pieces of furniture: a small table, a chair, a hard wooden bed. They are for CHRISTINE's *cell, made by her father. The bed is not complete. One side is down and needs to be dovetailed to complete the frame, after which the boards must be hammered into position.*

(NOTE: What follows is based upon the recorded ceremony for enclosing anchoresses. Poetic licence is taken. But Scene I must be performed in full, as a real church service, so that an audience is saturated in an intense religious atmosphere and feels itself witness to the ceremony of immurement. All the words of the service have relevance to what's happening and should be delivered as text, not mumbled.)

HENRY, *Lord Bishop of Norwich, enters followed by* MATHEW DE REDEMAN, *rector of the church, and then* CHRISTINE's *parents,*

WILLIAM *and* AGNES, *followed by* CHRISTINE'*s ex-fiancé,*
ROBERT LONLE, *followed by an old villager,* MATILDE, *and two
others, a* VILLAGER *and the* BISHOP'S CLERK. *A strong smell of
incense is in the air.*

MATHEW *prostrates himself before the altar and begins the
service, intoning:*

MATHEW. Psalm 6 which is David's:

> O LORD, rebuke me not in thine anger,
> neither chasten me in thy hot displeasure.
>
> Have mercy upon me, O LORD; for I am
> weak: O LORD, heal me; for my bones are
> vexed.
>
> My soul is also sore vexed: but thou, O
> LORD, how long?
>
> Return, O LORD, deliver my soul: oh save
> me for thy mercies' sake.
>
> For in death there is no remembrance of
> thee: in the grave who shall give thee thanks?
>
> I am weary with my groaning: all the night
> make I my bed to swim; I water my couch
> with my tears.
>
> Mine eye is consumed because of grief; it
> waxeth old because of all mine enemies.
>
> Depart from me, all ye workers of iniquity;
> for the LORD hath heard the voice of my
> weeping.
>
> The LORD hath heard my supplication; the
> LORD will receive my prayer.
>
> Let all mine enemies be ashamed and sore
> vexed: let them return and be ashamed
> suddenly.

> > (*During this beginning* AGNES *stands before
> > her daughter and begins to unbutton her
> > dress. She is so distressed that she cannot*

*complete the task, and sobbing is taken aside
by her husband,* WILLIAM.
Instead, MATILDE, *the old villager, takes
over and soon the girl is in a white chemise.
Another* VILLAGER *stands by with*
CHRISTINE's *habit in his arms.
The service is continuing meanwhile.
Everyone responds to the psalm.*)

ALL. Glory be to the Father, and to the Son, and to the Holy
Ghost; as it was in the beginning, is now, and ever shall
be, world without end. Amen.

MATHEW. Psalm 131 which is David's:

> LORD, my heart is not haughty, nor mine eyes
> lofty: neither do I exercise myself in great
> matters, or in things too high for me.
>
> Surely I have behaved and quieted myself,
> as a child that is weaned of his mother: my
> soul is even as a weaned child.
>
> Let Israel hope in the LORD from
> henceforth and for ever.

ALL. Glory be to the Father, and to the Son, and to the Holy
Ghost; as it was in the beginning, is now, and ever shall
be, world without end. Amen.

(CHRISTINE *prostrates herself.* BISHOP *and* RECTOR *stand
before her.* BISHOP *holds a cross in front of her.* MATHEW
*sprinkles her three times with holy water, then three times
with incense.
They raise her up. Two lighted tapers are placed in her
hands.*)

BISHOP. 'Go, my people, enter into thy chamber, shut thy
doors upon thee, hide thyself a little, for a moment,
until the indignation pass away.'

MATHEW. 'At that time Jesus entered into a certain town,
and a certain woman named Martha received Him into
her house, and she had a sister called Mary, who, sitting

also at the Lord's feet, heard His word. But Martha was busy about much serving, and she stood and said, Lord, hast thou no care that my sister hath left me alone to serve? Speak to her, therefore, that she help me. And the Lord answering, said unto her, Martha, Martha, thou art solicitous and troubled about many things. Now one thing is necessary. Mary hath chosen the best part, which shall not be taken away from her.'

(BISHOP'S CLERK *who is standing by with a chasuble presents it to the* BISHOP *who puts it on.*)

BISHOP. O God, who dost cleanse the wicked and willest not the death of a sinner, we humbly beseech thy majesty that in thy goodness thou wilt guard thy servant, Christine, who trusteth in thy heavenly aid, that she may 'ever serve' thee and no trials may part her from thee. Through our Lord Jesus Christ.

ALL. Amen.

(CHRISTINE *moves forward, places her candles above the altar, steps back, reads her profession from a document.*)

CHRISTINE. I, sister Christine, offer an' present myself to the goodness of God to serve in the order of an anchoress, an' according to the rule of that order I promise to remain henceforward in the service of God through the grace of God and the guidance of the church an' to render canonical obedience to my spiritual fathers.

(*She folds the document. A pen is handed to her. She scratches the sign of the cross upon it. Kneels before the altar.*)

BISHOP. O God, who dost quicken thy servant who has turned from the vanity of the life of this world to the love of thy heavenly calling, cleanse the thoughts of her heart, and pour upon her thy heavenly grace, that trusting in thee, and guarded by thy mighty power, she may fulfil that which by thy grace she has promised, and the work of this life well done, she may attain at last to that which thou hast vouchsafed to promise to those who trust in thee. Through Christ our Lord.

ALL. Amen.

(CHRISTINE *is helped on with the rough habit as the* BISHOP *intones*:)

BISHOP. May God put off from thee the old woman with all her works, and may God clothe thee with the new woman, for you who yearn passionately for union with her God are created in righteousness and true holiness.

ALL. Amen.

(CHRISTINE *prostrates herself before the altar. The* BISHOP *and* CONGREGATION *continue in subdued tones to chant the hymn of Pentecost in Latin: see last page.*

WILLIAM, AGNES *and* ROBERT *break away to the workshop. She to cut bread and pour ale for them; they to finish making the bed.*)

ROBERT. I know her passions. They have more to do with her than with heaven.

AGNES. Why, why, why? Someone say! I ask her, she tell me, but I understand narthin'.

WILLIAM. An' it's just you who should!

AGNES (*ignoring that*). 'All right,' I say, 'you want to retreat, but what need to be so severe? Fastin', beatin', prayin'! Hours and hours on end. Weave!' I tell her, 'Mend the church's clothes, collect for the poor, minister the sick, comfort the grieving! But this?!' An' she tell me, she say — with a scorn she get from I don't know who but I guess (*looking at her husband*) — she say: 'There's weakness in good deeds, mother. You just want me to have holidays from suffering.' So I begin to yell at her then —

WILLIAM. Tryin' to be the right mother at the wrong time!

AGNES (*ignoring that too*). I yell at her: 'But where be the virtue in sufferin'? The Divine spark is offended by sufferin', it is! Offended by it!' 'Nay, mother,' she tell me, 'your words is wrong way round. *Life* offend the Divine spark, which can only be found in heaven, an'

15

thaas what I prepare myself for.' 'That reveal me narthin',' I yell at her. 'I don't understand narthin' of all that!'

WILLIAM. 'Cos there ent narthin' so powerful as an idea whose time's come.

AGNES. 'Heaven! Heaven! The truth is revealed in heaven,' she yell back at me. Huh! 'If heaven is where all truth is revealed,' I tell her, 'then it must be hell!'

ROBERT. An' I reckon that were me to blame. Must have loved her wrong. 'Don't wanna marry you, wanna marry Christ,' she tell me.

AGNES. No, it's him. (*Meaning William.*) He's to blame. Had her taught words and grammar.

WILLIAM. She nagged for it.

AGNES. Where did the idea come from?

WILLIAM. I don't know, woman. But I know this, she was strange from birth an' grew stranger. An' who made her grow stranger? Who took her away from the love of fairs an' runnin' an' dancin' which rightly belongs to young girls? Who talked her silly about angels an' heaven an' hell an' the suffering of the Lord Jesus Christ?

AGNES. That's our way. No mother does different.

WILLIAM. But no other mother has a daughter lock herself up in small rooms for months on end. Too much piety in the house! More passion than a child should take.

AGNES. But I warned against books.

WILLIAM. Too late, woman, the child was called.

AGNES. By the devil, called.

WILLIAM. She'll miss them fairs.

AGNES. An' the tumblin' an' the jugglin' an' the wrestlin'. Blust! she love all that.

WILLIAM. There! A table an' chair for I don't know what.

AGNES (*mumbling on and quoting her daughter*). 'Change, change! There must be change!'

WILLIAM. And a hard bed to prevent her sleepin' too well.

ROBERT. Suppose we must be thankful she didn't ask for a coffin to sleep in.

(*They place the chair and table on the bed and carry all to and through the hole in the wall. Soon they return as the intoning of the hymn comes to an end. The ceremony continues over the prostrate* CHRISTINE.)

MATHEW. O God, who willest not the death of a sinner, but rather that she should repent and be cleansed, we humbly beseech thy mercy for this thy servant who has forsaken the life of the world, that thou wouldst pour upon her the help of thy great goodness that, enrolled among thy chaste ones, she may so run the course of this present life that she may receive at thy hand the reward of an eternal inheritance. Through Christ our Lord.

ALL. Amen.

(MATHEW *goes to the altar, plucks up one of* CHRISTINE's *candles, saying:*)

MATHEW. May the sacraments that we have received, O Lord, make us pure, and grant that thy servant, Christine, may be free from every fault, so that she whose conscience by sin is accused may rejoice in the fullness of pardon from on high. Through our Lord.

(MATHEW *turns, hands taper to* CHRISTINE. *The* BISHOP *takes her hand, the others form a procession behind. They move towards the hole. A litany is sung. When it is over and they are in front of the opening to the cell –*)

BISHOP. Let us pray. Hearken, O Lord, to our prayers, and let the clear light of thy presence shine upon this house. Let a full measure of thy blessing fall upon those who dwell therein by thy grace, that, dwelling in all sobriety in these temples made with hands, they may ever be temples of thy Spirit. Through Christ our Lord.

ALL. Amen.

BISHOP. Let us pray. Hear us, O Lord, Holy Father, eternal God, that if there be any thing against us or opposed to us in this house of thy servant, Christine, it may be cast out by the power of thy divine majesty. Through our Lord Jesus Christ, thy son, who with thee liveth and reigneth, in the unity.

BISHOP. Let us pray.

(CHRISTINE *stands before her cell. The* BISHOP *intones his prayer. At the same time* WILLIAM, AGNES *and* ROBERT *turn aside, and talk among themselves. We hear their words against the background of the prayer.*)

AGNES. How will she wash when she sweat an' she bleed? She'll die of her own smells, the mad girl. Her odour will poison her.

WILLIAM. No more games for you my gal, your runnin' an' dancin' days is over now, all your fleet an' sweet days, daughter.

ROBERT (*angry*). She've seen blue skies, she won't forget that. She've seen the mare matin', she won't forget that. She've seen the lamb skippin', the calf suckin', the sun settin', the rivers runnin', an' she've caught trout with me an' seen me naked, an' once touched me, an' she won't forget that.

BISHOP. Bless, O Lord, this house (*genuflect*) and this place, that in it may dwell health, holiness, chastity, power, victory, devotion, humility, gentleness, meekness, fulfilment of the law and obedience to God, Father, Son, and the Holy Ghost. And let a full measure of thy blessing (*genuflect*) rest upon this place and upon all who dwell therein in thee, that, dwelling in all sobriety in these temples made with hands, they may ever be temples of thy Spirit.

BISHOP. Through our Lord Jesus Christ thy Son, who with thee liveth and reigneth in the unity of the Holy Spirit one God.

(*The* BISHOP *takes* CHRISTINE *into the cell, saying:*)

BISHOP. The Kingdom of the world –

(*Enter.*)

18

ALL.– and all the glory of it have I despised for the love of my Lord Jesus Christ, whom I have seen, whom I have loved, on whom I have believed, whom I have chosen for myself.

(*The* BISHOP *returns.* MATHEW *and* CLERK *now slowly block up the entrance. It is a chilling sight. As it is being done:*)

BISHOP. Let us pray. We beseech thee, O Lord, to defend this thy servant, and through the intercession of the Blessed Virgin Mary and all the company of heaven, increase in her thy manifold gifts of grace, that being set free from the temptations of this world, she may have help in this life, and in the world to come everlasting joy. Through Christ. Let us pray.

Almighty God, unto whom all hearts be open, all desires known, and from whom no secrets are hid, cleanse the thoughts of our hearts by the inspiration of thy Holy Spirit, that we may perfectly love thee and worthily magnify thy holy name. Through Christ our Lord.

ALL. Amen.

BISHOP. Let us pray. Almighty and everlasting God, guide us, we beseech thee, in all our doings with thy most gracious favour, that in the name of thy beloved Son we may worthily serve thee in all good works. Who with thee liveth and reigneth in the unity of the Holy Spirit One God, for ever and ever.

(*The cell is now walled up. All turn and leave, chanting some Responsorium with its versicle concerning the saint in whose name and honour the church is founded – St James. Empty.*
Silence. Then – a song is heard. CHRISTINE *is singing to herself, very sweetly, calmly.*)

CHRISTINE.   I will forsake all that I see
　　　　　　　　Father and friend and follow thee
　　　　　　　　Gold and goods, riches and rent

Town and tower and tenement
Playing and prosperity
In Poverty·for to be one with thee.
(Between many of the scenes, like punctuations of comment, will be heard — loud or soft, vicious or sympathetic — the chanting of children. Like a street game.
Now we hear it, tenderly.)

VOICES. Christ-ine, Christ-ine, had a revelation yet? Had a vision, had a word, had a revelation yet? Christ-ine, Christ-ine, had a revelation yet? Had a vision, had a word, had a revelation yet?

SCENE II

Loud scream from a man. RICHARD LONLE *is dragged into a centre space by a* BAILIFF. *His hands are tied behind his back. He kneels with his back to us. The* BAILIFF *carries a brazier of hot coals with an iron poking from it.*

BISHOP *and* MATHEW *appear. It is some months later.*

BISHOP. You know what's to happen, Richard Lonle?

LONLE. Hypocrites! You preach labourers should be freed from all estates except your own!

BISHOP. We think it's better it takes place here, before the Church, as warning to others.

LONLE. The law says if I live in a town for a year an' a day I've earned my freedom.

BISHOP. You were caught before then.

LONLE. Three days! Three more days!

BISHOP. And why should you have wanted to leave? The manor made you, fed you, rented you land, guarded you in sick times. Was I a bad lord? Were you ill treated? Was my bailiff here unfair? And in these times! When

20

labour is desperately needed on the estate! You run away. *You* behaved unfair. And for why? To claim freedom! Freedom! No man's free! We're all bound by duties and responsibilities. So (*indicating branding iron*) you know the justice of this. I want you to understand the justice of this punishment.

MATHEW. (*Reads from the manorial roll. His heart's not in it.*) Richard Lonle, bondsman to the Manor of Henry Lord Bishop of Norwich, you did hold twenty-four acres of land for which rent of fourpence an acre was due, also three hens at Christmas and fifteen eggs at Easter. Further, you were bound to perform two days ploughing in the year, four half days mowing grass, two half days for hoeing, six days in autumn for reaping, and one day for your horse and cart to carry corn. You were charged with absconding from your local place of work and domicile, withdrawing your services, and dispersing your family, for which a right and proper jury found you guilty. By grace of his Lordship the Bishop Henry of Norwich, you have been granted the return of your house and land on condition of renewed service but that you be branded with hot iron upon the forehead as sign to your neighbours and before God that you have broken your bond.

BISHOP. Bailiff.

(MATHEW *holds the victim, and turns away in horror. The* BAILIFF *plucks the hot iron and brands* LONLE *on the forehead.*

He screams, faints. BAILIFF *drags him away.*

BISHOP *and* MATHEW *move up into the church.*)

BISHOP. They wanted him hung but I wasn't having any blood-letting, besides we're short of labour. You think I shouldn't even have had him branded, don't you?

MATHEW. The times change and the Church should follow, my Lord Bishop.

BISHOP. The Church will decide if times change.

MATHEW. With respect, the Church didn't call down the plague to decimate the population and rob labour from the land.

BISHOP. Rector, whatever vicissitudes God calls down upon us he will have his Church obeyed. Now more than ever. No matter what the master of Balliol declares. You're a Wycliffe man too, aren't you? (*Contemptuously*.) Each man holding dominion from God! The man doesn't know what he's talking about! Wants to do away with the power of the priests. Wants to do away with you, rector, what d'you say to that? Individual conscience! Have every man acting according to his own dictates and you'll have chaos. First thing God did he made order out of chaos and then he established the Church to preserve that order. The Church is *his* order and it will be obeyed! I'm sorry, I talk loudly. Unsettled times. I wasn't made for them. Don't even understand them. Not an intellectual background like yours, rector. Just worked hard, learnt the words, did my duty, and developed a passion for the land. Leave the divine inspiration to others, Henry, I say to myself, just administer. You love the earth and its seasons like a mother its child and tempers. Enough! Know your limitations and administer what you love. And I'll tell you something else. (*Indicates cell*.) I don't approve of them, either. How is she?

MATHEW. She says her prayers, eats little, advises from her window, confesses through her quatrefoil. In the beginning her confessions were full of guilts for small sins. Now, after six months, a little impatience seems to have crept in. She confesses to anger that the 'old life' still clings to her and she hasn't found the new one yet.

BISHOP. After six months? Huh! Tantrums and fervours – not always easy to distinguish between them and the real thing. But you insisted. 'She's called, my Lord Bishop, it's her vocation, my Lord Bishop. She's in communication with the angels my Lord Bishop.' Pah! (*Grumbling as he goes off.*) I've always warned – there's some can't bear the touch of God so they scream loud hymns and prayers to drown him out. Tantrums and fervours, tantrums and fervours!

SCENE III

Light up on a cell wall and window. ROBERT *outside* CHRISTINE'*s cell.*

ROBERT. It's not God's call you're servin' but some private devil.

CHRISTINE. Still bitter with me, Robert? Don't be that.

ROBERT. God didn't make you for that hole, he made you for the world which he made for you. The Bible says it.

CHRISTINE. In here is the world. I'm beginnin' to see it. The whole world. Out there you got clutter, you see narthin'.

ROBERT. There's cruelty, p'raps, an' unreason, an' death. But that ent God callin' you, thaas man drivin' you.

CHRISTINE. If you love me, Robert Lonle, pray for me an' don't taunt me.

ROBERT. You explain this, an' you explain that, but your words is wind an' mist, an' black meanin' white an' white meanin' black!

CHRISTINE. Month after month. The same complainin'. I don't have no other words.

ROBERT. Try village words, an' fairground words.

CHRISTINE. Them's for villages an' for fairgrounds!

ROBERT. Then I'll keep askin'. Again an' again an' again.

CHRISTINE (*after a pause*). There is – a marvellousness in it. To be alone, minute after minute after minute after minute after minute. Takes my breath away. Such power, such strength, such freedom. An' no fear.

ROBERT. In the silence an' the dark?

CHRISTINE. In a silence that speaks an' a dark what's light.

ROBERT. There you go! Wind an' mist an' black is white! You make no sense, Christine.

CHRISTINE. Don't come no more if I make no sense. You're a torment.

ROBERT. Sorry, then.

CHRISTINE. It's love, Robert. I can't say no more than that. I'm filled with love for a man what took upon hisself great sufferin' an' torment an' death. To redeem us to God's grace. He suffered. For *us*. Thaas a powerful knowledge. Can't you see the powerful pity thaas there? It make me weep. An' when I weep I know I got to share a tiny part on it. (*Pause.*) I hear tell a story, once, of a mother an' son who lived near high mountains. As the boy grew he were drawn to them high mountains. A spirit moved him to climb them while his mother begged him, no! She feared for him, see? But the day come when he knew his strength an' he climbed an' he climbed. An' his mother watched him go. An' the days passed, but he never come back. An' though that mother went through great anguish an' pain yet she marvelled at his courage an' she were proud. But as time passed she could think of narthin' but his pain. It tormented her. Till one day she resolved to trace her son's steps. She'd adored him, see. Life meant narthin' without him. She needed to be with him. She had to travel his road up that mountain, to share his pain, to share his fate. There were no other way.

(*Sounds of taunting children.*)

VOICES. Christ-ine, Christ-ine, had a revelation yet, had a vision, had a word, had a revelation yet?

ROBERT. Get off! Get away with you! Get off! Off!

(*But we hear them again, at a distance.*)

VOICES. Christ-ine, Christ-ine, had a revelation yet, had a vision, had a word, had a revelation yet?

SCENE IV

Carpenter's workshop. WILLIAM *and* ROBERT *are answering the questions of the* TAX COLLECTOR *who's writing on sheets propped on a sawn tree-trunk.*

COLLECTOR. Name and age?

WILLIAM. William. Forty-two.

COLLECTOR (*writing*). Willelmus. Wife?

WILLIAM. Agnes. Forty.

COLLECTOR. Agneta. Children?

WILLIAM. One. Christine.

COLLECTOR. Cristina. How old is she?

WILLIAM. There'll be no tax for the crown from her, she give all to God.

COLLECTOR (*sceptically*). Is that so?

WILLIAM. You've not been told of her? She've made these parts famous enough.

COLLECTOR. Ah! The anchoress. A rebuke to rudeness and self-indulgence. Very chastening. But I must confess, nothing can make me lose my sins and shames and temptations. Some I control, some have a power I'm not built to control. What's to be done? Nothing, I say, but guard against excesses and be what of a good man I can, and God can spit wrath and indignation as he will, there's an end, for I can do no more.·

WILLIAM. There speaks someone from the city.

COLLECTOR. Right! The solitary life is not one *I'd* be fit or excited for, but I'm full of reverence and awe, full of it. You must be proud.

> (*But his tone is casual. The men are silent. The* TAX COLLECTOR *looks around, then at* WILLIAM *for confirmation.*)

WILLIAM. Aye, carpenter.·

COLLECTOR. Carpentarius.

ROBERT. He say one thing you write another.

COLLECTOR. Latin, young man. They may preach sermons
in English these days but tax returns must still be
recorded in Latin. And who are you?

WILLIAM. My apprentice.

ROBERT. You'll know of me from my father, Richard Lonle.
You were there yesterday. Alice my mother, two
brothers Edmund an' Henry, two sisters Joan an' Clare.

COLLECTOR (*looking through sheets*). Lonle, Lonle. Ah.
Ricardo, agricole, Alicia, Edmundo, Henrico, Johanna
and Claricia. And you must be Roberto. (*Smiles*.) Latin!
And you're all bondmen to the Bishop's Manor.

ROBERT. Now. But next year us'll buy our liberty.

COLLECTOR. Is that so? Now, possessions? And I want to
hear everything. You know the penalty for hoarding.
Although – arrangements can be made, eyes closed,
this and that ignored. (*Smiles*.)

WILLIAM (*coldly ignoring invitation of bribe*). Three saws, two
axes, a spokeshave, two adzes, two hammers, four
oxen, seven steers, two cows, two-and-a-half quarters
of winter wheat, five quarters of oats . . .

SCENE V

WILLIAM's *voice dies away as* CHRISTINE's *voice from the cell
takes over.*

CHRISTINE. There was a oneness time. I search that. When I
were with my soul, an' my soul were with my body, an'
my body were with me, an' we was all one with God an'
His lovely nature an' there were O such peace an'
rightness an' a knowin' of my place. That really were a
oneness time that were. An' I search that, Lord Jesus.

(*Now old* MATILDE, *the busybody and gossip, enters and
places her stool beneath the window, cards her wool, and
chatters.*)

MATILDE. You crossed your mouth?

(CHRISTINE *grunts her replies.*)

MATILDE. Good! An' your eyes an' ears an' your breasts?
Good! For as the advice goes – an anchoress must love
her window as little as possible, especially a young 'un.
There's men in this village with lewd eyes an' soft
tongues, an' there's boys with taunts, an' old women
with useless prattlin'. Your mother bring you your
food? Good! Now here's a story about a Belgie saint
called Yvetta, tell me by a smithy who heard it from a
nun who heard it on a pilgrimage to Rome which is
how I get all my stories being a collector of stories 'bout
saints which you'll be one day if you work hard at it.
Yes! Get them from all over. Pilgrims. Vagabonds. Ole
cooks at the fairs who I growed up with but thems also
old an' widows now. Full o' stories. So, Yvetta. Sweet
an' pretty thing she were, an' happy, but poor gal, she
had to marry. Howsomever, when her husband die she
renounce the world and go to serve in a leper colony
where she so much wanted to be a leper herself that she
eat an' drink with them, look, an' even wash in their
bath water! Blust! You shouldn't catch *me* doin' that!
An' when she were enclosed she were visited by that
many temptations that she had to hev a haircloth on her
an' an iron chain with two heavy tablets hanging round
her neck, an' added to them she give her poor ole limbs
a whole lot o' floggin', there! She didn't eat too much,
neither. Baked flour an' powdered ashes three times a
week! An' all her day an' nights were spent in prayers,
tears, genuflections an' striking of the breast, an' when
she sleep that were on sharp pointed stones. An' she die
exactly on the day she *say* she were goin' to die. Hands
outstretched an' eyes raised to heaven. Seventy she was.
An' they say that even though it were the middle of the
winter wi' a great storm of wind an' hail an' snow, yet
the birds gathered round her cell an' sang as if it were a

summer day. An' her face was all a brilliant glow, they
say.

SCENE VI

Inside the church. MATHEW *by the quatrefoil taking confession
from* CHRISTINE.

CHRISTINE. . . . Oh all you blessed angels an' saints of God!
Pray for me a most miserable sinner that I may now
turn away from my evil ways, that my heart may
henceforward be forever united with yours in eternal
love, an' never more go astray. Amen. I've sinned,
father.

MATHEW. Tell me your sins, my daughter.

CHRISTINE. My suffering's not true, father.

MATHEW. That doesn't sound like a sin, Christine.

CHRISTINE. I find pleasure in my cell. Time passes quickly
an' I look forward to each next day.

MATHEW. Pleasure is not a sin, either.

CHRISTINE. But not sufferin' enough *is*! I want my chains, I
want my haircloth.

MATHEW. You *want*, you *want*! Those are sins! The Bishop is
deciding.

CHRISTINE. He've been decidin' for months.

MATHEW. Be careful, Christine. Don't enfeeble the body or
you'll not be able to sing the praises of God.

CHRISTINE. You don't understand, father. My flesh. It needs
mortification. I can concentrate on narthin'. I need pain
to help me in my contemplations. Please.

MATHEW. How can you contemplate if you mutilate your
body? The pain will intrude.

CHRISTINE (*contemptuously*). Are you a priest or not? Will you help me or not?

(MATHEW *is anxious. He is weak, she is wilful.*)

MATHEW. What harmony can your thoughts know through torn flesh?

CHRISTINE. There ent no harmony without sufferin'. Sufferin' is what our Lord went through, how can I know him without sufferin' also?

MATHEW. Suffering can only bring knowledge of suffering.

CHRISTINE (*impatient anger*). I'm dirtied! Unclean! Selfish! Wilful! I must destroy that selfish will.

MATHEW. To which end you are using the most extra-ordinary power of will!

(*He stops suddenly, realising he's arguing against the entire concept of the solitary pursuit which the Church has sanctioned. He's caught in a moment of doubt which* CHRISTINE *senses. She's a powerful personality of which he's afraid.*)

CHRISTINE. Are you fit to hear my confessions, father? You sound to me like you've become a very strange priest.

MATHEW. It is written that, the life of solitude is a wilder-ness, and in this wilderness are many evil beasts, the serpent of venomous envy, the bear of sloth, the fox of covetousness –

CHRISTINE. – the swine of gluttony, the scorpion with the tail of stinkin' lechery! I know them!

MATHEW. And the lion of pride, and the unicorn of wrath! (*Pause.*) I will come another time. You sound out of temper today.

(*He leaves. She calls after him.*)

CHRISTINE. Bring me my haircloth an' chain, father. Bring them!

VOICES (*taunting*). Christ-ine! Christ-ine! Had a revelation yet? Had a vision, had a word? Had a revelation yet? Christ-ine! Christ-ine! Had a revelation yet? Had a vision, had a word? Had a revelation yet?

SCENE VII

Carpenter's workshop.

WILLIAM *and* ROBERT *at work on a wheel.* AGNES *and* MATHEW *alongside.*

AGNES. Here's your bread an' some meat from the fair, an' some bean an' bacon soup which is good for you. (*Pause.*) And here's the Bishop's priest. (*Meaning: who is not good for you. Pause.*) No! I aren't leavin'!

MATHEW. It's about Christine.

    (*Awkward silence. The men don't know whether to eat or not.* AGNES *decides for them.*)

AGNES. Eat up, look. That'll be cold presently.

WILLIAM. Worried about our daughter are you? Speak to *her*, then. (*Pointing to Agnes.*)

MATHEW. I urged the Bishop, it's true. Even against his doubts. But I believed she was called.

AGNES. You believed your church would look better in the district with an anchoress to boast of.

MATHEW (*attempting sternness*). My church is your church and you remember I'm the Vatican's choice for this parish, granted me by Pope Urban himself –

    (*But his feeble authority touches their stony defiance not one bit. He relents. He's a good man really.*)

    (*Gentler.*) She's asked for haircloth and chains.

AGNES. An' she'll get them. Somehow. An' go on to crueller things. I know her.

MATHEW. There's such a powerful hold on her mind.

ROBERT. Ent that what you want?

MATHEW. The solitary life is a search for union with God, it should bring release.

AGNES. Instead of imprisonment by stubbornness you mean?

ROBERT. By love, *she* say.

MATHEW (*dismissively*). Love's an intoxicant. It's like hate.

Its juices ferment emotions that cloud the truth of
things. Love can make you feel great good is done to
you, hate can make you feel great harm is done to you
when neither is the case.

WILLIAM (*curious about him now*). An' *you* approved of her
going in, father?

(MATHEW *is troubled. Every time he speaks he seems to
surprise himself. Is he moving away from the faith? Is he a
Wycliffe man? He is fearful he will say too much to the
wrong people.*)

MATHEW (*leaving*). I promise I'll keep close to her.

ROBERT. Well he didn't stay long!

AGNES. I should've offered him food.

WILLIAM. *Is* he the Vatican's choice? I hear tell he were chose
by some Italian priest who couldn't find time to see after
this parish 'cos he had six others to attend to, look!

(*Now moonlight falls on* CHRISTINE's *cell as she whispers
desperately to herself.*)

CHRISTINE. A showing! A showing! Give me Jesu Lord my
lovely Christ a showing! Touch me with your passion.
Any sign will do. That crucifix before me. Bleed!
Weep! Smile! Whisper to me! A showing! A showing! I
crave a showing, to stay with me every dark day of my
dark life in this dark cell!

SCENE VIII

CHRISTINE's *cell.* MATILDE *arrives, places her stool, cards her
wool, and chatters.*

MATILDE. You crossed your mouth? Good! An' your eyes
an' ears an' breasts? Good! Your mother brought your
food? Good! Now here's a story. Saint Veridiana. Born

two hundred years ago they tell me, place called Siena in Italy. This one fasted even as a child, an' wore a chain an' hairshirt! *Her* cell were ten feet long an' only three an' a half wide. No furniture, narthin', just a ledge in the wall an' two snakes for company. She tell her Bishop they were sent in answer to a prayer that she be allowed to suffer similar to what St Anthony did, 'cos you know *he* were tormented by devils in the form of wild beasts. They say them snakes sometimes lashed her insensible with their tails. They killed one just before she died, the other never returned. In summer she slept on the ground, an' in winter on a plank with a piece of wood for a pillow, an' now she wore an iron girdle an' a hairshirt. Only one meal a day she had, sometimes bread an' water, sometimes boiled beans, most times narthin' 'cos she give it away to the poor what used to come beggin' every night. 'Course, she don't talk to no one but the poor an' afflicted you know. An' she live like that for thirty-four years. Till she were sixty. Then she die. She also knew exactly *when* she were goin' to die 'cos she sent for her confessor, an' closed her windows. An' at the very moment she die all the church bells began ringin' by theirselves, look. An' when they pulled down the wall there she was, dead on her knees, with her psalter open at the Miserere! (*Pause.*) Is that another comin' to your window? (*Shouting.*) Go off there! That ent the right time o' day to be callin'. (*To* CHRISTINE.) My, they do come don't they! All wonder an' excitement an' reverence. Think 'cos you cut yourself off from life you hev a special secret for it! (*Shouting.*) Get away, I say! (*To* CHRISTINE.) You livin' solitary make *them* uneasy. Ha! The church may be your anchor, gal, but she need *you*, that she do. (*Calling.*) You're persistent. What's up, then? (*Pause. She listens. Then to* CHRISTINE.) It's a young gal. No more'n about twelve. Says she wants to know how it begin for you.

32

(*Long pause.*)

CHRISTINE. I hear rumours, little gal. My soul hear rumours. Rumours like whispers, thaas how it begin for me. (*Pause.*) Them weren't rumours in words but in – senses. Feelin's. Them were feelin's like rumours that another place up there existed. I don't talk of heaven, not rumours of heaven but – how shall I describe it for you? Rumours of another kind of knowin'. I couldn't make things fit but rumour come to me that it had to. I couldn't walk with myself but rumour come to me that I could. I didn't love myself but rumour come to me that I was loved. So they must come from somewhere I say to myself, an' I listen hard an' follow the sound to find the truth. Sometimes I get so eager an' excited that I think I'm there. But thaas only the echo I come to, not where the sound come from, an' that make me rage and weep an' I have to start again. (*Pause.*) Rumours, little gal, rumours, beware the echoes but wait for the rumours.

(*Pause*)

MATHILDE (*collecting herself, speaks to 'gal'*). There! You got that? Rumours! You wait for the rumours. Beware the echoes but wait for the rumours. (MATHILDE *leaves, shrugging, utterly lost.*)

SCENE IX

Carpenter's workshop. February 1379.

WILLIAM, AGNES, ROBERT *and* TAX COLLECTOR.

COLLECTOR. Now be sensible. You're not the only one's got to pay this new tax.

AGNES. The king had money off us two year ago, look.

COLLECTOR. *You've* only got to pay twelve pence a head but the rich 'uns have to pay up to twenty shillings a head, and even the clergy are being called on for six shillings and eightpence. Except the lower orders. They only have to pay twelve pence. If they're over sixteen.

(*He's become increasingly fearful of their mood.*)

But you know my policy. Someone got six in the family and I only count five, and we split twelve pence. Saves six pennies. That's not to be sneezed at. (*Pause.*) If you don't work with me the King's men will send more officers with greater powers and it'll be imprisonment for the lot of you.

(*Silence. He tries authority.*)

Right! My good nature's at an end. This money's needed for the safety of the realm and support of the army abroad in its wars. Now –

WILLIAM. The wars in France.

COLLECTOR. Yes, them.

WILLIAM. Disastrous wars. Losin' wars. Costly, disastrous, losin' wars.

COLLECTOR. Well, I don't know about that. I'm paid to collect taxes not judge how they're spent.

ROBERT (*threateningly*). We hear news from Kent that a tax collector raped a farmer's daughter.

COLLECTOR (*frightened*). Well that's in Kent and that's him, and this is Norfolk and this is me.

ROBERT. The farmers hung 'im.

AGNES. I do believe he's shittin' hisself!

SCENE X

Interior of church. Empty. We hear CHRISTINE *at her prayers.*

CHRISTINE. . . . We adore thee, O Christ, an' we bless thee, because of thy holy cross Thou hast redeemed the world. We adore Thy cross, O Lord. We commemorate Thy glorious passion. Have mercy on us, Thou who didst suffer for us. Hail, O holy cross, worthy tree, whose precious wood bore the ransom of the world. Hail O –

(*She stops abruptly. Ecstatic joy enters her voice.*)

Oh! Oh! A showing!

(*She can hardly believe it.*)

A showing! A showing! I have a showing! There before me!

(MATHEW *rushes in.*)

It's a shape. The world's shape. I see its joins, what holds it together. I see the claspin's an' links. *There*'s a dovetail. *There*'s a mortise an' tenon. *There*'s the hole an' there's the dowel. Oh! Oh! Mountain, river! Sun, storm! Clay, harvest! I see the harvest grow. I hear the flower blossom. I know the colour of the wind, the dark in light. There, there, before me, all joined an' locked an' fittin' an' rhymin'. There-is-no-mystery! A shape, a shape, I know the shape! Oh blessed merciful Jesus Christ, I prayed to the cross, an' the tree, an' the precious wood, an' you give me a showing.

(MATHEW, *by way of cautioning her, now intones a warning.*)

MATHEW. Beware, my sister, beware the vision. Awake, asleep, dreaming, beware the vision. Illusions! They could be illusions. Satan has many stratagems. Once he made a man believe he was an angel and that his father was a devil, and he made him kill his father. Beware, Christine. (*Long pause.*) Christine, are you all right?

CHRISTINE. The dark in the light? I said 'the dark in the light'. I *did* say 'the dark in the light', didn't I? (*Pause.*) That were no showing, then. (*Pause.*) Though it did make sense. Gone. An' I nearly named the parts.

(*Pause.*)There's a foul stench in my cell. Arrgh! Who'll rid my cell of its foul stench?

 (*Long pause.*)

MATHEW. Christine? Christine? Are you all right, Christine? Shall I confess you?

CHRISTINE (*hissing*). Go away.

 (*Sad taunting voices of the children.*)

VOICES. Christ-ine! Christ-ine! Had a revelation yet? Had a vision, had a word, had a revelation yet? Christ-ine! Christ-ine! Had a revelation yet? Had a vison, had a word, had a revelation yet?

SCENE XI

Carpenter's workshop. May 1381.

 WILLIAM, AGNES, *and* ROBERT. *It's evening, dim. They sit over a pint of ale.*

AGNES. I hear plans an' plottin's in the villages around.

WILLIAM. There need to be. No more grazin' places, an' forbid to hunt an' fish which we done for years, look!

ROBERT. An' a third tax comin'.

AGNES. They're after the Manor documents. Them!

WILLIAM. Burn them an' they won't have record of who's tied to who, for what, nor where, nor narthin'!

ROBERT. Good rid on 'em, too.

AGNES. The documents an' rolls of the Priory at Carrow, thaas the first place they're after. Then the Manor House of the Duke of Lancaster at Methwold. Him next.

WILLIAM. You know a lot don't you, woman?

AGNES. Can't depend on you to know what's goin' on can I? Someone in this family's got to keep an ear to the world

36

or we'd all be lost.

ROBERT. What more d'you know, missus?

AGNES. I don't know, I just guess. There'll be killin's.

WILLIAM. Don't see no sense in that.

AGNES. You sit on people you squash sense out of them, don't you?

ROBERT. A third tax! Want their heads examined!
    (MATHEW *enters*.)

WILLIAM. Come to share some ale, father?

AGNES (*fussing*). Sit you there, look. I'll see to him. (*She pours*.)

MATHEW (*to Robert*). I'm afraid I've disappointing news, Robert.

ROBERT. I know what that'll be.

MATHEW. The Bishop won't grant permission for you to take up grammar.

ROBERT. 'Course he won't!

WILLIAM. Your father's got the money ent 'ee?

ROBERT. No matters how much money my father've got, the Bishop 'ont take it. The yearly levy, thaas what he'll take. Ploughin' his lands, shearin' his sheep, maltin' his grain – thaas what he'll take. An' when we grind our corn in his mill an' must leave some, he'll take that! An' when we brew ale in his brewery an' must leave some, he'll take that! An' when we bake bread in his ovens and must leave some he'll take that! 'Course he 'ont let me study grammar. Us study, us'll leave!

AGNES. An' be branded with hot irons on your forehead like your father.

ROBERT. That was then. Now he've got an acre or two and he's savin' to buy his freedom an' he want me to read, an' my mother want me to read, an' my brothers an' sisters want one in the family an' they see my talent for it an' *they* want me to read, an' now that they tell us English is takin' over from French in the church an' the parliament an' the courts an' the schools – *I* want to read! An' if she hadn't put herself away she'd 've *taught* me to read.

(*They all sit in silence a while.*)

MATHEW. It's not in her to be solitary.

ROBERT. I could've told you that.

MATHEW. She sits there *waiting* for visions. At once! Now! Immediately! After only three years when there's some have waited sixty and seen nothing.

AGNES. First thing, she rise, crosses herself, kneels on that bed you made her, bows and stays like that through one prayer, then another, then more. Then she dresses, still prayin', mumblin', mumblin' – not that she has much to dress in to. Used to give her a clean shift each day, then she wanted one each week, now she tell me she only want one each month, an' soon it'll be a year, an' the filth an' the smell an' the hardship an' pain an' misery – an' for what, I ask, for what? (*She's crying.*) Oh my poor gal, my poor my own gal.

MATHEW. And she knows that if she gives up there's only excommunication and hell.

WILLIAM. Don't sound to me like it's in *you* to be a priest, neither.

MATHEW. Not for this church.

SCENE XII

CHRISTINE'*s cell.* MATILDE *arrives, places her stool, cards her wool, and chatters. But now a distressed and wild* CHRISTINE *mocks and mimics her familiar opening sentences.*

MATILDE. You crossed your mouth?

CHRISTINE (*mimicking*). You crossed your mouth?

MATILDE (*surprised but impervious*). Good! An' your eyes – ?

CHRISTINE. An' your eyes?

MATILDE. An' your ears?

CHRISTINE. An' your ears?

MATILDE. An' your breasts?

CHRISTINE. An' your breasts?

MATILDE. Good!

CHRISTINE & MATILDE (*together*). Your mother brought your
   food?

MATILDE. Good!

   (*But she does a double-take. Something* is *wrong. Waits.
   Will* CHRISTINE *continue to mock her?*

MATILDE. Now here's a story.

   (*But she's uncertain* what is *wrong or what to do. She'll risk
   what she's always done, however.*)

MATILDE. My favourite. You'll like this one. Saint
   Christiana. Another Belgie, an' she weren't an
   anchoress or narthin', she were just – well, holy! A
   spirit! A real spirit who could climb trees an' church
   towers an' was so thin an' light from livin' in the
   wilderness that she could sit on the thinnest branches of
   trees, look, an' sing psalms! There were three sisters,
   three on 'em, an' she were given the job o' lookin' after
   the cows. But did she mind? 'Course she didn't. She'd
   sit out there contemplatin' an' contemplatin' and
   contemplatin' so much that she put herself into a trance.
   Yes, a trance! An' that were so deep they all thought she
   was dead so they took her to church to be buried. But
   half way through mass she get up off her bier an'
   clamber up the walls to the roof, look! an' she don't
   come down till her mass is finished an' the priest
   promise to absolve her. An' when she do come down
   she tell 'em all how when she were dead she were shown
   purgatory, hell an' then paradise, an' they give her the
   choice o' remainin' in heaven or sufferin' on earth for
   the conversion o' sinners. She come back! Cor, that
   congregation fled! 'Cept for her eldest sister who was

too terrified to move. Glorious life she hed. In an' out o'
the wilderness, livin' on herbs, prayin', contemplatin',
prophesyin', hevin' ecstasies. Like a sparrow she was,
very weird and wonderful.

(CHRISTINE *shrieks loudly. Three times.*)

SCENE XIII

Inside the church. June 17 1381.

A TRAVELLING PRIEST *is giving a 'sermon'. But not to the
audience.*

PRIEST. 'Blow ye the trumpet in Zion, and sound an alarm
on my holy mountain.' Thus saith the prophet Joel.
There are new sermons being preached in our land,
brothers and sisters. Here's one for you: each man hath
his own conscience! God give it him! Each man!
Dominion over himself! Therefore turn to your priests
and tell them, tell them this: not one vicar be upon the
earth but many. Each man is a vicar unto himself. For
look, if it were not so we'd be dead and dull things with
no power to think at all. But we must think hard
enough how to make the day live, eh, brothers?

'Beat your plowshares into swords, and your
pruning hooks into spears: let the weak say I am
strong.' Thus saith the prophet Joel. One hundred
thousand men are gathered under Wat Tyler, brothers.
Canterbury has opened her gates, the manor-court
records are burnt, they've slaughtered the lawyers in
Blackheath, and dragged mad John Ball from prison to
sing another sermon. Have you ever heard John Ball
sing, brothers and sisters?

'Good people,' he sings, 'good people, things will
never go well in England so long as goods be not in

common. By what right,' sings he, 'by what right are they who we call Lords greater folk than we? They are clothed in velvet, and warm in their furs and ermines, while we are covered with rags! But,' sings John Ball, 'when Adam delved and Eve span, who was then the gentleman?' D'you like those songs, brothers and sisters? Them's the songs being sung from the coast of Kent up here to the Wash.

'And it shall come to pass afterwards that I will pour out my spirit upon all your flesh; and your sons and your daughters shall prophesy, your old men shall dream dreams, your young men shall see visions.' Thus saith the prophet Joel. And –

(BISHOP HENRY *storms in.*)

BISHOP. In my church? Blasphemy and treason in my church?

(*Comic chase.* PRIEST *dodges here and there with confident fun, throwing out slogans and rhymes of the day.*)

PRIEST. 'Help truth and truth shall help you!'

BISHOP. Who gave him permission? Who let him in? (*Calling.*) Bailiff! Rector! Who opens God's house to the wandering blasphemer?

PRIEST.

> Now reigneth pride in price
> And covertise is counted wise
> And lechery withouten shame
> And gluttony withouten blame.

BISHOP. Bailiff! Rector! I'll have you hung, drawn and quartered! You'll burn in hell!

PRIEST (*fleeing*). 'God do bote,* for now is tyme!'

(*The* BISHOP *puffs after him.* CHRISTINE *screams again. Three times.*)

CHRISTINE (*a voice of dread*). I do not have the vocation! Release me! I do not have it!

*God do 'bote' = God 'claims'.

SCENE XIV

Inside the church. Lit away from the cell wall. BISHOP *and*
MATHEW.

BISHOP. Knew it! From the start! Wrong! I felt it, warned it!
But you insisted. 'She's called, my Lord Bishop, it's her
vocation, my Lord Bishop!' And now, on top of
everything else, farmers and knights and Wycliffe's
mad Lollard priests on the rampage. They're burning
records in the Manor Houses, d'you know that? How
can we keep track of who's bonded to who, now? And
in the midst of all that a girl raving to be absolved from
the most sacred of vows. You satisfied?

MATHEW. There must be a hearing, my Lord.

BISHOP. Who says so? I'll say what must and must not be.

MATHEW. We must be seen to be considering the pleas.

BISHOP. I've considered them. She took the vows of
poverty, chastity and obedience, and she'll keep them.
A vow is a vow!

MATHEW. Perhaps she can be moved, share a life with
another anchoress.

BISHOP. A vow is a vow. She wanted unity with God? She
wanted to reach the perfect state? On her head be it! A
vow is a vow!

MATHEW (*persistent*). Her parents and the apprentice Robert
Lonle are waiting to see you.

BISHOP. Well send them away! I trust not her, not him, not
any of them. Their heads are full of discontent and
confusion, and their tempers are insolent.

MATHEW. But what shall I tell them?

BISHOP. Tell them! Tell them! Tell them they neglected to
plough and harrow my lands in the spring. Tell them
God's granted my corn to grow and they owe it to God
and me and the land to reap and make hay and grind.
Tell them that! A struggle, why is everything a struggle?

MATHEW. I'll call them in, my Lord.

(MATHEW *leaves*. BISHOP *glares in the direction of* CHRISTINE's *cell*. MATHEW *returns with* AGNES, WILLIAM *and* ROBERT.)

BISHOP. And was she an aggravation for you, too? Did she have tantrums as a child? But you thought they were visions, didn't you? Thought you had a special little girl, so you indulged her? Fanned her fervours, inflamed her imagination?

WILLIAM. That were mother's doin', makin' her so pious.

MATHEW (*worried they'll squabble*). But with the church's blessing. Come, William, she's your wife.

AGNES. I don't mind him. He'll quarrel anywhere. An' I'm not behind with it myself! It was him had her taught readin'.

BISHOP (*exploding*). Reading? Reading? Did you ask permission? Was the levy paid for it? Did you take leave of your senses? (*To Robert*.) And *you* want my permission to learn the grammar! (*Pointing to the cell*.) See where reading leads? To notions that take power over minds too weak to control them. Notions have lives of their own, with hands to grab you, arms to hold you, chains to bind you! (*Pause to collect his temper*.) What have you come to ask of me?

AGNES. She's our only child, Lord Bishop, sir. No sons to help our work, to look after us in old age, to bring us grandchildren. Thaas a hard life on earth, an' the promise o' heaven then an' a family now – them's the only relief in it. She've given three years to our Lord Jesus Christ. She've tried to please God an' the Church. Let them be pleased enough, Lord Bishop, sir, your reverend. Let her go.

WILLIAM. There's no gain in a reluctant solitary, my Lord. You want the folk what's under your wing to take strength an' examples from your anchoresses, don't you, sir? They must be shinin' lights, give courage, set a

standard? What standard can my poor daughter set?
She've gone in there lookin' to fill her head an' heart but
she've emptied them instead, she've got no standards to
set. She's no more use to the church, your Lordship. Let
her go.

ROBERT. She were betrothed to me for love of me, an' I to
her for love of her. There ent a week passed in all these
three years I've not sat with her, an' she talk an' she talk
an' she talk, an' she talk, an' I know she love me still. Let
her go, sir. Let her go an' we'll be married. You'll hear
narthin' of us more if you let her go.

(*Pause.*)

BISHOP. We will think on it.

(*The* BISHOP *and* MATHEW *leave, followed by the other
three.*

*Now a red glow slowly grows, like a house burning, as we
hear the children's voices.*)

VOICES. Christ-ine, Christ-ine, had a revelation yet, had a
vision, had a word, had a revelation yet? Christ-ine,
Christ-ine, had a revelation yet, had a vision, had a
word, had a revelation yet? Christ-ine, Christ-ine . . .

CHRISTINE. Not fit! Not fit! Christine not fit! You have hell
anchored to your church, Bishop Henry. Break down
its walls, break them, break them. In the name of God
BREAK THEM DOWN!

(*Sound of drums and marching feet. They grow louder and
louder, topped by the cry of a man being slaughtered.*

*The red glow lingers. Light shifts from church to carpenter's
workshop.*)

SCENE XV

Carpenter's workshop.

AGNES seems to be anxiously waiting for someone.

The TRAVELLING PRIEST enters carrying the dead ROBERT in his arms. Lays him gently in wood shavings. The PRIEST is himself in tatters and blood.

AGNES gasps, bends to wipe away blood, her low moaning continues throughout.

PRIEST. In London, the Friday after the feast of Corpus Christi, the boy King met Wat Tyler at Mile End, and agreed to his demands. I watched it happen. The King bowing to the people. Exhilarating. Cold shivers down my spine as the roar and the cheer went up. Then the mood changed. They got intoxicated. At the tower they beheaded Sudbury, Hales and the King's physician, which intoxicated them more, and the crude and rough ones surface like scum to the top and begin paying off old scores and murdering the aliens. I shouted and warned but there was quick and easy tongues to call me traitor. At Smithfield we give the King a second set of demands. 'Come to us and talk,' he says. I stood and warned, no! but the tongues were quick and easy. Wat Tyler stepped to the other side where the Mayor of London killed him, and that was that! The Charters of Freedom were withdrawn, John Ball sang his last sermon and was hung drawn and quartered at St Albans, and the rest come home. (*Pause, looking at the dead boy.*) One way or another.

(CHRISTINE *is heard singing her song, but sadly now.*)

> I will forsake all that I see
> Father and friend and follow thee
> Gold and goods, riches and rent
> Town and tower and tenement

Playing and prosperity
In Poverty for to be one with thee.

(*Light transfers to inside the church.*)

SCENE XVI

Inside church. Lit away from cell wall.

BISHOP *and* MATHEW *confront* WILLIAM *who is on his knees before them awaiting the verdict.*

BISHOP. We cannot. It is not in our power to sanction the breaking of a vow, nor can we bless an adultress to Christ. She cannot leave the cell.

(*Now the cell wall revolves slowly. We see the inside of the cell. Backed against the wall is* CHRISTINE. *The sight of her is shocking. She is dirty, unkempt and terrified as her eyes take in what she now realises is to be her cell for ever.*)

VOICES (*distant*). Christ-ine! Christ-ine! Had a revelation yet? Had a vision, had a word, had a revelation yet? Christ-ine! Christ-ine! Had a revelation yet? Had a vision, had a word, had a revelation yet?

(*And on the chanting the lights slowly fade.*)

ACT TWO

One continuous scene – in parts. Interior of CHRISTINE's cell.

Part 1 – CHRISTINE *in the corner of her cell, terrified.*

CHRISTINE. I ent narthin', I hev narthin', I desire narthin', save the love of Jesus only. I ent narthin', I hev narthin', I desire narthin' save the love of Jesus only. I ent narthin', I hev narthin', I desire narthin' save the love of Jesus only. I ent narthin' . . .

Part 2 – CHRISTINE *on her knees before her crucifix.*

CHRISTINE. Oh Lord Jesus Christ whose flesh were dug with holes into which you bid us creep for comfort – comfort me. Comfort me an' help me an' have mercy on me, Lord. Have mercy an' help me. I ent saint nor martyr but a feared little thing, a poor, feared little thing wi' thin soul an' weak heart an' no strong body like I thought. I tried, Lord, wi' all I got I tried. But that ent in me. That just ent. I give what I had but that weren't as much as I thought. I thought I heard you speak to me an' sign me a path, but that were the devil, Lord, the devil givin' me ideas bigger'n what I were made for. Oh Jesus, Jesus, Jesus. Your father made me, he know what I am, what I'm fit for. Speak to him, Lord. Tell Him to make a sign to the Bishop Henry. Tell Him what you see. Look at me an' tell Him how I bein't made for the solitary life. I bein't, Lord. I bein't, I bein't, I bein't, I

47

bein't, I bein't, I bein't . . .

Part 3 – CHRISTINE *in the corner of her cell.*

CHRISTINE. I ent narthin', I hev narthin', I desire narthin'
save the love of Jesus only. I ent narthin', I hev narthin',
I desire narthin' save the love of Jesus only. I ent
narthin', I hev narthin', I desire narthin' save the love of
Jesus only. I ent narthin' . . .
*(Sounds of taunting children outside grill window of cell.
Their hands come through, hoping to touch her. She ignores
them, sits on in her corner. Their chanting takes over from
hers.)*

VOICES. Christ-ine, Christ-ine, had a revelation yet? Had a
vision, had a word, had a revelation yet? Christ-ine
Christ-ine, had a revelation yet? Had a vision, had a
word, had a revelation yet, Christ-ine, Christ-ine . . .

Part 4 – CHRISTINE *by the quatrefoil.*

CHRISTINE. Yes, father, I know I begged to be a solitary, I
know I did. Raged even. Thaas right, I did. But now I
must return among people. You stay there, father, an'
I'll tell you. Thaas like this here. When I'm alone, in the
silence, in the dark, I see the truth – an' thaas noisy.
'Tis! Noisy! Full o' people pullin' an' pushin' different
ways – 'I'm this, I'm that, that be right, this be right,
gimme this, gimme that, do that, do this!' All screamin'
through the air, an' I can't stop 'em, I can't rub 'em out,
so I think – if I'm *among* people, *with* 'em, look, I'll only
see a few, I'll only hear a few. Stands to reason, father.
Honest. Believe me. The solitary hears the truth an'
thaas more'n she can bear. No one's made to hear *all* the
truth, father. Help me, please. I shall go mad with the

noise. What good'll I be to God then? Poor, little mad gal? Eh, father? God don't want no poor, little mad gals, do 'ee? So help me, then. Help me, help me, help me . . .

Part 5 – CHRISTINE *in the corner of her cell.*

CHRISTINE. I ent narthin', I hev narthin', I desire narthin' save the love of Jesus only. I ent narthin', I hev narthin', I desire narthin' save the love of Jesus only. I ent narthin', I hev narthin', I desire narthin' save the love of Jesus only. I ent narthin' . . .

Part 6 – CHRISTINE *is lying flat on her back on her bed. After many, many seconds she sits bolt upright, swivels round, her face alight with a new thought.*

CHRISTINE. There ent one God, there's two! (*Pause.*) What sense do it make to give trouble before gettin' to heaven when you can get people into heaven wi' no trouble? There must have been two Gods. Workin' to make the world at the same time. Like one man diggin' earth out of the hole an' another shovellin' it back in! (*She's incredulous at the thought. Then panics!*) Oh Lord Jesus Christ, which 'un do I pray to?
   (*She moves to the crucifix, then away from it, then to it, then away, uncertain which end of the cell to go to. Finally she chooses the one she knows, and desperately kneels before crucifix.*)
Hail Mary, full of grace! The Lord is with thee, blessed art thou amongst women, an' blessed is the fruit of thy womb, Jesus. Hail Mary, full of grace! The Lord is with thee, blessed art thou amongst women, an' blessed is the fruit of thy womb, Jesus. Hail Mary, full of grace!

The Lord is with thee, blessed art thou amongst
women, an' blessed is the fruit of thy womb, Jesus. Hail
Mary . . . (*Stops suddenly.*) Thaas a blasphemous
thought, Christine Carpenter. Two Gods! Where'd a
thought like that come from? (*Returns to lying flat on her
bed. Long silence. Then –*) Two Gods, two Gods. One
diggin', the other shovellin'. Two Gods, two Gods.
One diggin', the other shovellin' . . .

Part 7 – CHRISTINE *paces up and down her cell.* BISHOP *and*
MATHEW *are talking with her through the quatrefoil. They can't
be seen by the audience.*

CHRISTINE. Two Gods, two Gods! One diggin', the other
shovellin'! Two Gods, two Gods! One diggin', the
other shovellin'!

BISHOP. Be still, child. Sit. Take hold. You are a bride of
Christ. He'll comfort you. Trust Him. Now, are you
sitting on your stool? The one your father made
specially for you with his loving hands? You're loved,
Christine. Loved and admired.

CHRISTINE (*sitting on stool*). Not fit.

MATHEW. The villagers look up to you.

CHRISTINE. Not fit.

MATHEW. They're proud of you, their very own anchoress.

CHRISTINE. Not fit.

BISHOP. Control yourself, child! I have questions for you.
Be calm. Think carefully. Have you told people of your
vision?

CHRISTINE. Yes.

MATHEW. 'Yes, my Lord.'

CHRISTINE. Yes, my Lord.

BISHOP. And it's your own vision, no one put it to you?

CHRISTINE. No, my Lord.

BISHOP. Have you had fevers recently, sickness?

CHRISTINE. No, my Lord.

BISHOP. You don't have to keep saying 'my Lord', only the first time. Have you memories of such notions from the past?

CHRISTINE. The vision's mine! Alone! It come to me fresh an' burnin' bright. *For* me. For the world. There be two Gods!

BISHOP. That's heresy!

CHRISTINE (*hardly restraining her glee*). Not fit, let me go, not fit, not fit!

BISHOP. Do you still love Christ?

CHRISTINE. Yes! Yes!

BISHOP. Do you still long for union with God?

CHRISTINE. Not fit! Not fit!

BISHOP. Then was it not a temptation of the devil?

CHRISTINE. No! No! He tell me. There's a God of love an' a God of hate. One is good an' one is evil. Like one man diggin' earth out of the hole an' another shovellin' it back in. An' each had a son. I am one, He say, an' Satan's the other, He say. An' all what you see around, an' all what's been, an' that ever will be was created by the two on 'em, an' that's the truth, He say. For look you, no God of *love* could put *evil* in your heart, could He? That'd be a careless God wouldn't it? (*Pause.*) Wouldn't it?

BISHOP. It's rubbish! She's seen two Gods? Possible, but unprovable! It's as convenient a way of describing the workings of this damned life as any.

MATHEW. Just as the teaching of our Church is?

BISHOP. Except that it is our Church and the one in power with responsibility, and I want that Church obeyed, respected and strong. Order is order, duty is duty, a vow is a vow! And I think you'd do well to find another parish.

MATHEW. Or another Church!

CHRISTINE. Not fit! Not fit! Christine not fit! Christine have union with hell not heaven. You have hell anchored to your church, father. Break down its walls, break them, break them. In the name of God BREAK THEM DOWN!

Part 8 – CHRISTINE *is by the window grill.*

CHRISTINE. Thaas no good comin' to me for advice, little gal. What advice can a miserable sinner like me give anybody? Go to the Bishop Henry, or the rector, or my mother an' father. They'll give you good advice. (*Pause.*) Oh no, you mustn't go thinkin' 'cos I live here that I'm anyone special, I just –

(*She thinks. Then changes her mind and decides to offer advice.*)

Hear me then. When you die your soul go to the terrors you've been afeared of all your life. You had no terrors then your soul's left in peace. You hev them – they go with you! So you live that you should hev no terrors, little gal, you live like that, look.

(*Pause. The taunting voices of children return. Their hands poking through the grill, close to her face. She stands, wild-eyed, listening to the words, transfixed by the waving hands, her teeth clenched tight.*)

VOICES. Christ–ine, Christ–ine, had a revelation yet? Had a vision, had a word, had a revelation yet? Christ–ine, Christ–ine, had a revelation yet, had a vision, had a word, had a revelation yet? Christ–ine, Christ–ine . . .

(*They give up. She relaxes a little. Struggles to collect herself.*)

CHRISTINE. Well, thaas an improvement. I spoke to somebody. Give 'em advice. Didn't know what I was talkin' about but I spoke, leastways. So there, now. (*Pause.*) So there, now. (*Pause. Looks left and right.*) So there, now.

(*She* must *establish a routine. She runs to kneel before crucifix and begins fast praying.*)

CHRISTINE. Hail O Cross, dedicated to the body of Christ, and adorned with his limbs as with pearls. O Cross, O victorious Wood, true salvation of the world, peerless among trees in leaf an' flower an' fruit, medicine of Christians, save the sound an' heal the sick. (*Striking her breast hard.*) Let what cannot be done by human power be done in thy name. (*Genuflecting each time.*) We adore thee. We adore thee. We adore thee. (*With thumb she makes a sign of the cross on the ground and kisses it.*) Hail Mary, full of grace! The Lord is with thee; blessed art thou amongst women, an' blessed is the fruit of thy womb, Jesus. Hail Mary, full of grace! The Lord is with thee; blessed art thou amongst women, an' blessed is the fruit of thy womb, Jesus. Hail Mary, full of grace! The Lord is with thee; blessed art thou amongst women, an' blessed is the fruit of thy womb, Jesus. Amen.

(*Pause. What next? She rises quickly and sits on her stool. Pause. What next? Rises. With the end of her dress she dusts the table, then stool, then the bed, then the stool again. Pause. What next? She places the stool in a different position. Then another position. Then in another position. Pause. What next? There is a hairbrush in her cell, under her bed. She reaches for that and begins furiously to bring order to her unkempt hair.*)

It's because you don't look after yourself, gal. Thaas why they don't trust you. They look through them holes an' they see dirt an' filth an' there's smells an' goodness knows what, an' they think they see a mad woman. So put yourself straight an' bring back the gal what made the village proud. The runnin' gal, the dancin' gal, the gal-at-the-fair gal! Ha! Ha! they listened to you then. 'Cos you was like them they didn't mind your ways an' your prayers for them an' preachin' them

an' your lockin'-yourself-up-to-suffer-for-them. So
pull your old self together, there's folk comin' to your
window for comfort an' advice. (*Moves to window.*) No,
little gal, I don't mind you comin' to talk to me. (*To
herself.*) You crossed your mouth? (*Crosses her mouth.*)
Good! You crossed your eyes, your ears an' your
breasts? (*Crosses them.*) Good! (*To the window.*) Now,
ask me. Ask away. (*Pauses. Listens. Laughs.*) Ha! Ha!
Ho! Ho! Thaas a big 'un, then. You're a bold 'un. The
meanin' of life? Ha! Ha! Thaas a big question for a little
gal. (*Gaily.*) There *ent* no meanin', little gal. None!
But – ha, ha! There's purpose! Simple! To do good. No
other. In a word, a deed, a chair made, a tree planted,
the poor fed, a wrong forgiven, in love . . . in
love . . . in love . . . for as 'tis written: 'An' God said
"Let there be light," an' there was light. An' God saw
the light, that it was good . . . an' God saw everything
that he made, an' behold, it was very good.' Love, little
gal, the purpose is to love. 'Cos the Lord Jesus Christ
loved you so much, look, that he suffer an' die for you.
Love, little gal. There ent narthin' more powerful than
that!

(*She is jubilant. Continues brushing her hair.*)

There! That weren't bad! I did well then. You did very
well, Christine. Narthin' mad about that. She'll go
away an' tell people that the gal Christine Carpenter
give her good words of advice, an' people'll start
comin' again, and the word'll spread, an' get to the
Bishop's ears, an' he'll write to the Pope, an' you'll see,
gal, you'll see, you'll see, you'll see.

(*Pause. What next? She runs to kneel before crucifix and
recites three Aves.*)

Hail Mary, full of grace! The Lord is with thee. Blessed
art thou amongst women, an' blessed is the fruit of thy
womb, Jesus. Hail Mary, full of grace! The Lord is with
thee. Blessed art thou amongst women, an' blessed is

the fruit of thy womb, Jesus. Hail Mary, full of grace!
The Lord is with thee. Blessed art thou amongst
women, an' blessed is the fruit of thy womb, Jesus.
Amen.

(*Pause. What next? She rises. Sits on her stool. Intones.*)

The remedy for pride is humility. The remedy for envy
is love. The remedy for anger is patience. The remedy
for sloth is work. The remedy for covetousness is
contempt for earthly things. The remedy for avarice is a
generous heart. The remedy for lust is mortification of
the flesh. (*Beats her breast, hard.*) The remedy for lust is
mortification of the flesh. The remedy for lust is
mortification of the flesh. The remedy for lust is
mortification of the flesh. The remedy for lust is
mortification of the fle-e-e-e-esh!

(*She shrieks last word. Rises and walks around beating
herself wildly, finally banging her head against the stone
wall, calling out at the same time.*)

CHRISTINE. Flesh flesh flesh flesh flesh flesh flesh flesh help
help help help help help help help mercy mercy mercy
mercy mercy mercy mercy mercy O Lord Jesus Christ
tell them tell them tell them I have no vocation I am not
fit I am not fit I AM NOT FIT! (*Stops abruptly.*) What
else can I do to show love?

(*Pause. What next? Long long pause to recover. Moves to
quatrefoil. Sits on floor.*)

Am I worthy enough to love him, father? Thaas what I
kept askin' myself. Till one day I say – no more
questions, only declarations. You think too much. You
got to pray, declare more. Don't ask, declare! So I did. I
love him I love him I love him I love him I love him (*and
on and on just past the moment when it can be borne no
longer*). There! An' now I see it. There it is. Before me.
My love. An' he smile. Like a teacher to a pupil what's
just discovered the answer. A tender smile. He
approves. Good gal! I knew you'd get there one day.

Oh, a blessed smile, a joyous, happy smile. Such a big smile that it make me want to laugh. To laugh. (*She does so, a full rich laugh.*) To laugh. Thaas the funniest thing in the world, ha, ha! To think I would never discover it. Ha, ha! It were so simple! All I had to do was say it. Ha! Ha! I love you I love you I love you I love you! An' there he were! Ha! Ha! Like a teacher! Ha! Ha! I knew you'd get there one day, he say. Ha ha ha! Oh! Oh! Oh! Ha! Ha! Oh! Oh! Oh!

(*Her laughter grows. At first a really rich, natural, infectious laugh. Then it becomes uncontrollable, hysterical. And stops abruptly.*

Pause. What next? Sits on her stool. Intones.)

The remedy for pride is humility. The remedy for envy is love. The remedy for anger is patience. The remedy for sloth is work. The remedy for covetousness is contempt for earthly things. The remedy for avarice is a generous heart. The remedy for lust is mortification of the flesh. (*Beats her breast.*) The remedy for lust is mortification of the flesh. The remedy for lust is mortification of the flesh.

(*Pause. What next? She rises, moves to a corner of the cell, hoists her dress, and urinates.*)

Part 9 – CHRISTINE *in the corner of her cell. She cradles the heavy crucifix in her arms. Laments and rocks backwards and forwards.*

CHRISTINE. The poor wail, the orphan sighs, the widow is desolate, the pilgrim needs water, there's danger for the voyager, hardship for the soldier, temptation for the nun, cares for the Bishop. Come to me, come to me, come, come, come, come.

(*Pause.*)

I've loved him from cradle-time. No smile like my baby's. See, they humiliate him now. *I* can't comfort him, though. I've loved him from his first falls. No cry like my baby's. See, there are thorns on his head. *I* can't comfort him though. Was anything so tender? The smell of oil on his skin, the trust in his eyes as I wrapped him warm. See, they've given his poor body a cross to bear. Why don't *my* bones crack instead? I can't comfort him though. And that first word he spoke! Such cleverness. How swift he learnt. See, they nail him now. My lovely boy, my own, my flesh, my blood. An' did I feed an' watch you grow an' guard you 'gainst the plagues for this? An' did we look at blue skies, an' the mare matin', an' the lamb suckin', an' the calf suckin', an' the sun settin', an' the rivers runnin', an' catch trout – for this? (*Cries out.*) Put nails through me! Through my hands, my feet. Me! Me! Oh the ache, the ache, the helpless ache. I can't bear it! Can't bear it! Cannot. Oh, oh . . .

(*Pause.*)

The poor wail, the orphan sighs, the widow is desolate, the pilgrim needs water, there's danger for the voyager, hardship for the soldier, temptation for the nun, cares for the Bishop. Come to me, come to me, come, come, come, come, come . . .

Part 10 – CHRISTINE *in the corner of her cell. She has exposed her breasts and, as she intones, her fingers move round and round caressing her nipples.*

CHRISTINE. The poor wail, the orphan sighs, the widow is desolate, the pilgrim needs water, there's danger for the voyager, hardship for the soldier, temptation for the nun, cares for the Bishop. Come to me, come to me, come, come, come, come, come, come, come, come . . .

Part 11 – CHRISTINE, *by the quatrefoil, her back to the wall.*

CHRISTINE. It's my thoughts, father, I can't put my thoughts on *him*. I see him on the cross, I see that sweet face sufferin', I see that poor body hangin' limp on its nails, an' I feel the pain. I feel it, here an' here an' here an' here an' here, an' I stand with my back to the wall, my arms outstretched (*her movements follow her words*) my eyes closed, an' I cry out 'Lord Jesus, sweet Lord, I'm with you, here I stand, I feel the pain, I'm with you.' An' then, an' then – Oh forgive me, father, forgive me! but as I stand, my arms outstretched, my eyes closed – new thoughts come (*her legs move apart now*) an' I can't turn them away 'cos they're O so sweet. I'm naked. My body open to the sky, my skin in the grass, sun on my breasts. I feel cool winds bring me the smell of the hawthorn and the wild mint. An' I see birds sweepin' an' singin'. An' those clouds, those glorious, rollin' shapes, that sweet scent, that soft air – thaas not the devil's forms, I say. Forgive me, father, but I say thaas never the devil's forms. An' I'm torn between shame an' delirium. The spring, father, the spring! I am crucified upon the spring!

(*The taunting chants of the children are heard. Their hands wave through the grill.*)

VOICES. Christ-ine, Christ-ine, had a revelation yet, had a vision, had a word, had a revelation yet? Christ-ine, Christ-ine, had a revelation yet, had a vision, had a word, had a revelation yet? Christ-ine, Christ-ine . . .

(*She stands with her back to the wall, arms outstretched, listening, watching the waving hands. Slowly she moves towards them. Watches. Then – she grabs one and plunges her teeth into it. There is a terrible scream. She releases the hand. The voices, screaming, move and die away.*

Long pause. What next? She looks around her cell. She turns to the wall, places her hands on it, then moves along it

58

*crossing one hand over the other, feeling the wall, even the
imaginary walls, her hands crossing over, in space, as in
mime, so that we 'see' the walls. And as she moves round her
cell in this way she mumbles to herself.*)

CHRISTINE. This is a wall, an' this is a wall, an' this is a wall,
an' this is a wall, an' this is a wall, an' this is . . .

(*On which poor, mad, imprisoned figure moving round her
forever small space the lights slowly fade till only a faint light
comes through her grill. Then – darkness.*)

Veni, Creator Spiritus,
Mentes tuorum visita,
Imple superna gratia
Quæ tu creasti pectora.

Qui diceris Paraclitus,
Altissimi donum Dei,
Fons vivus, ignis, caritas
Et spiritalis unctio.

Tu septiformis munere,
Digitus paternæ dexteræ,
Tu rite promissum Patris,
Sermone ditans guttura.

Accende lumen sensibus,
Infunde amorem cordibus,
Infirma nostri corporis
Virtute firmans perpeti.

Hostem repellas longius,
Pacemque dones protinus:
Ductore sic te prævio
Vitemus omne noxium.

Per te sciamus da Patrem,
Noscamus atque Filium,
Teque utriusque Spiritum
Credamus omni tempore.

Deo Patri sit gloria
Et Filio qui a mortuis
Surrexit, ac Paraclito
In sæculorum sæcula.
Amen.